Crazy Crocheting

Cartoon by Phil Garland

University Heights kids concentrating on their crochet projects

Crazy Crocheting

BY FERNE GELLER CONE

Photographs by J. Morton Cone & Ferne Geller Cone

LINE DRAWINGS BY RACHEL OSTERLOF

ATHENEUM   1981   New York

LIBRARY OF CONGRESS CATALOGING IN PUBLICATION DATA

Cone, Ferne Geller.   Crazy crocheting.

SUMMARY: Presents basic crocheting instructions and
emphasizes creating original designs by using unusual materials
such as cut-up newspaper strips.
Also includes instructions for special projects.
1. Crocheting—Juvenile literature.   [1. Crocheting.   2. Handicraft]   I. Title.
TT820.C7826   746.43′4   81-1275
ISBN 0-689-30867-1   AACR2

Published simultaneously in Canada by
McClelland & Stewart, Ltd.
Composition by Dix Typographers, Syracuse, N.Y.
Printed & bound by R. R. Donnelley & Sons Inc., Harrisonburg, Virginia
Designed by M. M. Ahern
First Edition

For Stephanie Rachel—with love

FGC

Contents

Crazy Crocheting

Two lopsided mugs—single crocheted wool. Made by Mary Lee Lykes

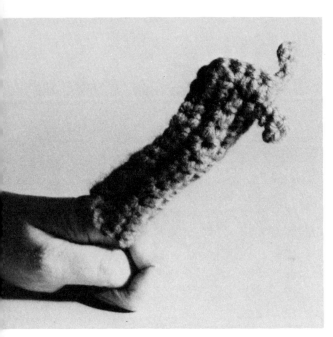

Snail with feelers. Crocheted by Margie

Hand carved crochet hooks—designed by Bill Dungan and Andi Dalton; photo by Anne Hinds

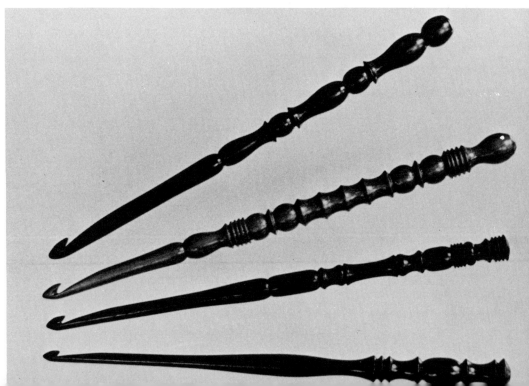

1

What Is Crocheting?

Doll purse made in Bolivia. Knit body with crocheted hats, hair, fingers and trim. Hand spun wool

A loop of yarn, string, or thread, pulled through another loop with a hook is called crocheting. A crochet hook looks like a little wand with a rounded hook at one end. With this hook and some yarn, pull one loop through another, and you can make all kinds of shapes—round, oval, square, oblong, squiggly. These shapes can look like mountains, trees, animals, and even people.

The first crochet hook was invented a long time ago. Someone discovered that a piece of wood or bone with a hook on one end could pull one loop of fiber through another. Eventually all those loops would become a piece of material. This piece of material could then be made into clothing. One person taught another how to use that tool, until lots of people learned. And that's how it all started.

In the old days, people crocheted things like bedspreads, placemats and fancy collars and cuffs. Usually these were crocheted from very fine cotton thread using a tiny crochet hook. Some people still do this. But crazy crochet is different. You can make

Napkin ring crocheted from fine plastic thread over a plastic ring. Made in Germany. Courtesy of Rachel Osterlof

fun things to play with or to display on a shelf or hang on a wall. You can even crochet interesting things to wear, too.

The yarn and hook will easily fit into a pocket or your purse, so you can carry your crocheting with you. When you have a cold and have to stay in the house and you're bored, pick up your crocheting and make something silly in a bright color. You'll feel better. It's fun to watch the material grow larger or smaller, or go around in circles.

When my daughter was about eight years old she was very sick and had to stay in bed for a long time. Reading or watching television didn't interest her any more, and we ran out of games to play. So I taught her how to crochet chains. She made whole bunches of chains, in lots of colors, all different lengths. When one color was used up, she would start a new one. It kept her busy just watching the chains get longer and longer.

Crazy crocheting is fun because it

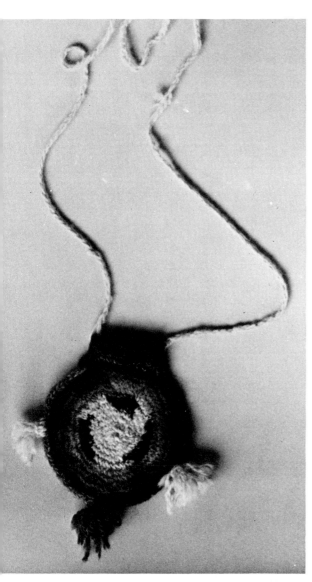

Circle purse made in Bolivia. Decorated with tassels, chain stitch shoulder strap, single crocheted of hand spun wool

doesn't matter what kind of yarn you use. It can be wool, ordinary string, nylon fishing line, rope—even strips of newspapers or cloth, or old nylon stockings cut into spirals. Anything that can be handled easily and worked with a crochet hook is useable. And if you don't have a crochet hook, your finger can be the hook. The stitches don't have to be perfect, and you don't have to count them either. If you make a mistake, cover it up or put a shell or rock in it.

The kids at University Heights School in Seattle learned to use their crochet hooks with all kinds of yarns and strings. One boy used plastic bread wrappers cut into narrow strips. Another student made a little blanket with every kind of leftover yarn she could find.

After the kids learned to handle the yarn and hook, they began to make up their own designs. They did some really weird stuff!

Look at the pictures in this book. Most of the examples were done by those Seattle kids. Once you learn to handle the crochet hook and yarn and learn a couple of simple stitches,

Michelle and Shana relaxing in the loft

Detail of single crocheted plastic bread wrapper strips

you'll be able to invent your own designs, too.

There's no limit to what you can make. Best of all, crocheting is very relaxing. You can dream with your eyes open while you are working along or listen to the radio, or talk with friends. Meanwhile your hands are creating something special.

Are you left handed? Not to worry. You can still learn to crazy crochet the same way right-handed kids do. My daughter is left-handed, but she was comfortable learning to crochet right-handed because she learned that way from the very beginning. Most cro-chet patterns are written for right-handed people. You work from right to left. So when you become more experienced and want to try following a printed pattern from a crochet book, it will be easier to follow that pattern. Otherwise everything will be backward.

There are only four simple stitches you need to know for crazy crochet—a chain, single crochet, double crochet and a slip stitch. Once these stitches

University Heights kids learning the basics from teacher

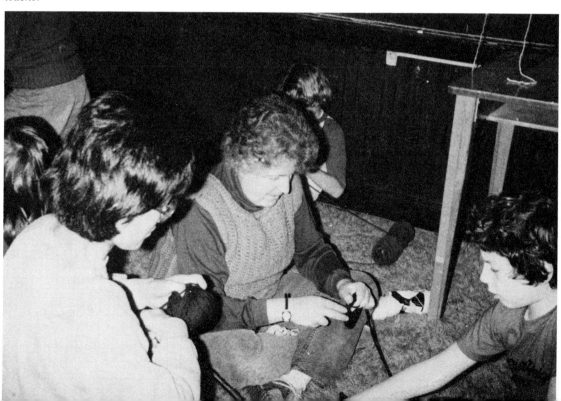

are learned you can make a whole bunch of crazy shapes.

Then you can make a wider shape by increasing or adding stitches. To make the shape narrower, decrease or subtract stitches. Add a new color at the beginning or end of a row, or right in the middle. That's OK. Start with a smooth, flat yarn, then change to a poufy yarn. Then change to plastic twine, if you want to.

While you are crocheting along add a goofy button, an old piece of jewelry, or even a feather. Do you have a junk drawer in your house? Rummage around and see what goodies you can find. Leave some big holes and fill them up later.

Best of all, when crazy crocheting, you don't have to measure unless you want to. So go find a comfortable place to sit. Be sure the light is good so you can see what you are doing. Follow the easy directions in this book, and pretty soon you'll be creating your own crazy crochet designs!

This is how you hold your fingers—Mother working with University Heights student

Everybody pay attention. Author working with
University Heights students

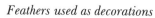

Feathers used as decorations

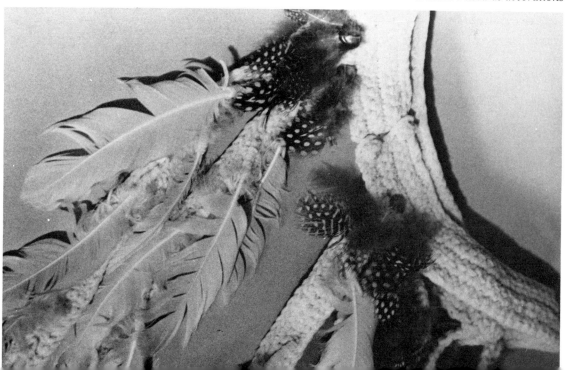

2

Crochet Hooks and Other Stuff

Crochet hooks come in lots of sizes and are made from plastic, metal, or wood. There are also crochet hooks in tiny sizes made from steel. All crochet hooks have pretty much the same shape—they look like little sticks with a hook at one end. The hooked end is used to catch the yarn. Crochet hooks cost about 30¢ to 60¢, depending on the size. Maybe you'll want to have a couple of sizes just to see how the stitches change with another size hook.

Buy a crochet hook at a yarn shop, a variety store, and at most places that sell sewing supplies. Maybe someone in your family already crochets and will let you borrow a hook. Then you won't have to spend any money.

Can you whittle? Try making your own crochet hook from a piece of wooden doweling. You can buy the doweling at a lumber yard for about a quarter.

In the beginning, while learning to handle the hook and yarn, try a medium size aluminum hook. It is lightweight and smooth, and very strong. Go to a shop and check out all the crochet hooks before you spend your money. Hold different kinds and sizes to get the feel of them.

Plastic hooks come in lots of sizes, too. They're not my favorite kind for crazy crochet because they can break easily. Besides, if you use a synthetic

Different sizes of crochet hooks

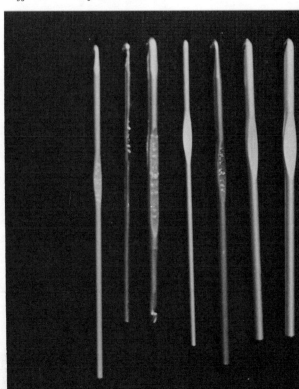

yarn with a plastic hook, sometimes the heat from your hands will make the yarn stick to the hook. Then you have to struggle to get the hook through the loops. But if you already have a plastic hook, try it out anyway. It's better than no hook at all.

The wooden crochet hook is usually made in larger sizes and the handle is a little longer than the metal or plastic hook. A wooden hook is useful for working with a really fat, thick, puffy yarn. However, a long hook is harder to handle when you are learning and your hands might begin to ache. Besides, you have to be careful because it breaks easily too.

Sometimes when a wooden hook has been used a lot, the wood becomes rough and the yarn catches on the rough wood. Then you have to stop crocheting and smooth the wood with sandpaper. What a nuisance!

If you want to try making your own wooden hook, here's what you'll need:

1 10-inch length of ½-inch wooden doweling
A sharp knife
1 piece of rough sandpaper
1 piece of very find sandpaper
Furniture oil
Some soft clean rags
An adult to help you with the carving

Find a flat surface to work on—the kitchen table is a good place. (Be sure to ask for permission.) Cover the surface with newspapers or an old sheet so you don't mess it up.

Use a pencil or marking pen and draw a triangle about ¾-inch down from one end of the doweling. With a sharp knife, carefully cut along the triangle marking and discard the wedge of wood. (If you already know

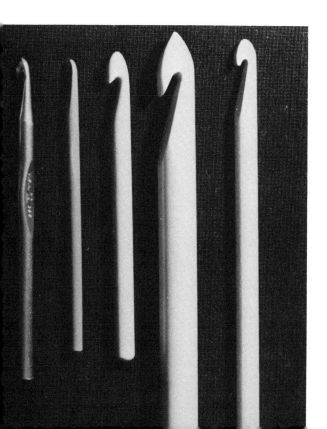

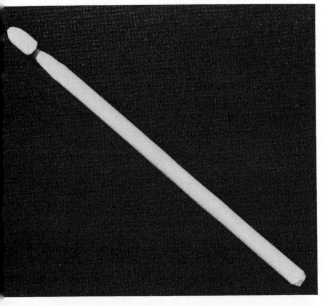

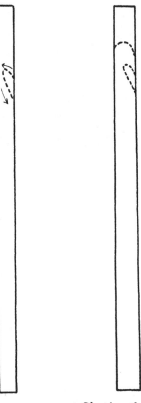

Piece of doweling

Shaping the hook

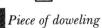

Marking the wedge

Upper left:

Home made crochet hook—front view

Lower left:

Home made crochet hook—side view

how to whittle you won't have any trouble, otherwise better ask an adult to help with the carving.) The doweling should look like the picture.

With the rough sandpaper, rub inside the notch until all the rough edges feel nice and smooth.

To round off the head of the hook, draw a curved line from the top of the carved notch around the top of the doweling. Smooth that end with the rough sandpaper. Keep checking the drawings to be sure your shape looks pretty much like them.

When you are satisfied with the shape, rub all over the hook with fine sandpaper until the wood feels very

smooth when you run your finger over it. Be sure there are no rough spots to catch the yarn. Now comes the last part. Use a clean, dry, soft rag, and carefully wipe the wood again. Be sure there is no sandpaper dust remaining. Moisten another clean rag with a few drops of the furniture oil. Carefully wipe every inch of the hook again. The oil gives the wood a nice shiny finish. Better wipe the wood another time to be sure any extra oil is wiped away. Roll the hook in another clean cloth and let it rest for a while. Any remaining oil will be absorbed by the cloth. Before using the hook give it another wipe. You wouldn't want to get oil on your yarn.

When you are all finished, gather up the newspapers and soiled rags and throw them away. And be sure to wash your hands.

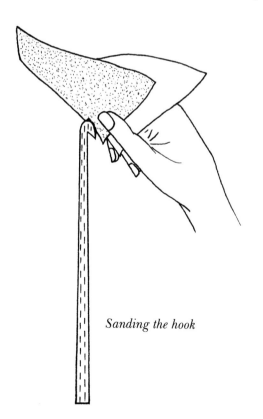

Sanding the hook

Other Handy Tools

There are a few other tools you will use from time to time for your crochet projects. They include some

T-pins, a blunt-pointed yarn needle with a big eye, a tape measure, and a pair of embroidery scissors.

The T-pins are for holding the parts in place when you want to connect them. The big-eyed yarn needle is necessary for sewing the parts together. Most of the time you won't need to measure your crazy crochet, but you should have a tape measure nearby just in case you want to. Use the scissors to cut the yarn.

T-pins, big-eyed yarn needle, tape measure, crochet hook, scissors

3

Yarns and Strings

There are hundreds of kinds of yarns, strings, and ropes you can use for crazy crochet projects. Some are smooth. When you crochet them the material will have a flat appearance. Some have a combination of big, thick, puffy parts with smooth parts in between. Other yarns have regular bumps. Still others combine bumps and smooth and lots of colors all mixed together.

Yarn used for crocheting clothing is stretchy and is usually wool or synthetic and sometimes cotton. Or it might be a combination of these. If you decide to crochet something to wear it's better to use something soft. For crazy crochet, almost anything you can work with a crochet hook, even string or plastic wrapping twine, is OK. Just be sure you can grab it easily with the crochet hook. Leftover

A variety of yarns . . . string, nylon fishing twine, knitting worsted, mohair, linen, cotton, jute

all the different yarns. Pinch and squeeze and ask the salesclerk to tell you about them. People who work in yarn shops are very helpful and will be glad to explain about yarns. Ask if there are some samples already crocheted so you can see how the yarn will look. You might want to buy a couple of kinds for practice to decide if they're fun to work with. If they're not easy to handle, or you don't like the feel, forget it. Try another kind. This way, you'll have a better idea what to expect when you start your special project.

Colors don't have to match (unless you want them to), so ask if there are some odd balls of yarn on sale. Many yarn shops keep a basket of odd balls tucked away in a corner. Usually they

Half-oval single crocheted from nylon pantyhose cut into strips

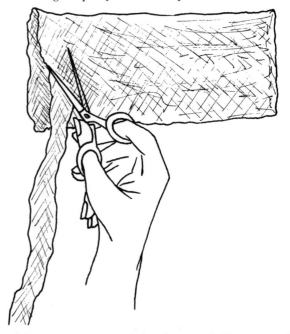

Cutting old pantyhose into strips

yarn scraps are perfect. Even narrow strips of material will work. Worn-out nylon pantyhose cut into spiral strips are fun to work with. Cut away the top and feet first.

Before deciding on a special project, go to a yarn shop and look at

Crocheted sailors' rope

are on sale for about half the regular price. Look through the basket until you find a yarn that looks as though it would be fun to experiment with. Then go home and try it out.

Plain string is worth considering for your first experiment. You can buy a ball of string at a variety or hardware store. It costs about 50¢ or 60¢ and goes a long way. Sometimes string comes in lots of colors, too. If you decide you don't like working with it, wind it back on the ball and give it to your mother to use for tying up packages. Don't throw it away!

Page 40 shows an example of several kinds of yarns and strings, all crocheted in single crochet stitch. Each is a different texture and color. They were crocheted with the same size hook and the same number of stitches on one practice piece. Notice how each section changed when a different yarn was used.

That's what's so much fun about crazy crochet—all the surprises.

4

Keep It Neat

It's easy to carry your crocheting with you. You can even stick it in your pocket. But it's a good idea to keep all your stuff in one place, in a special container, when you are not crocheting—like when you're outside playing with the other kids, or doing your homework. Then you always know where it is. Your mother will be happy that you are being so careful and neat.

Here's one idea you might want to try if you have an old school lunch box. Carefully wipe the inside and outside of the box with a *damp* cloth. Wipe it again with a *dry* cloth. Gather up scraps of sewing materials and cut them into lots of shapes—diamonds, rounds, or triangles. Paste the cut-out shapes all over the inside of the box. A white liquid glue is best for this. Be sure to cover the whole inside surface —even the inside of the cover. Trim off any loose ends with your scissors.

Instead of cloth scraps, use scraps of wallpaper or gift wrapping paper. Decorate the outside of the box, too. Paint it a snazzy color. Be sure the paint is completely dry, then paste some pictures of animals or football

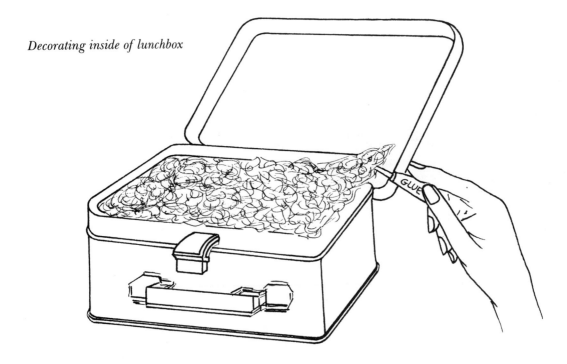

Decorating inside of lunchbox

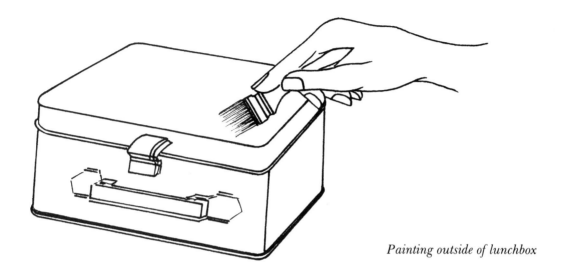

Painting outside of lunchbox

players or flowers on top of the painted surface. Paint stores have a quick-drying acrylic paint that goes on smoothly.

You don't have an old lunch box? Use a plastic bag. It's not as attractive, but it will keep your work neat and clean, and you can see what's inside.

5

Crochet Language

Beginning—beg
Chain—ch
Stitch—st
Chain stitch—ch st
Single crochet—sc
Double crochet—dc
Increase—inc
Decrease—dec
Skip—sk
Slip—sl
Slip stitch—sl st
Together—tog
Row—row
Round—rnd

When you learn to ride a bike, or play the violin, or even play a new game, there are usually some special words you need to know. Crochet has special words, too. Learn these words and you'll enjoy crocheting a lot more. Printed crochet patterns use signs to describe those words. They are often repeated many times in one pattern, so shortening the words uses up less space. For example: single crochet is "sc"; chain is "ch"; double crochet is "dc". When you see "ch 3, work 1 sc in every dc" it means to chain three stitches, work one single crochet in every double crochet.

I won't confuse you with too much new language, but here are some important words and their signs you should know right from the start:

There are a few important crochet phrases you should know, too. "Work even" means do not increase or decrease the number of stitches. When I tell you later on to "work even," just keep on working, without adding or subtracting stitches. This is true whether you are crocheting a tunnel, a square, or any other shape.

"Fasten off" is another important phrase. It means to lock the last stitch in place before you cut the yarn.

Sometimes in printed crochet patterns you will see an asterisk(*). When you see that sign, it means to repeat the directions from that sign until the next asterisk.

I talk a lot about markers. A marker is a piece of colored yarn tied into a stitch to remind you when to start a new row or round. A marker can also be a little safety pin, a paper clip, or even a bobby pin.

Crochet is a pretty easy language to learn, so go back and read the list again. Then start working with the crochet hook and yarn and see if you can remember the words as you experiment with each new step in crocheting.

1 ounce (oz.) = 28 grams (gr.)
1 inch (in.) = 2.5 centimeters (cm.)
1 foot (ft.) = 30 centimeters
1 foot (ft.) = 0.3 meters (m.)
1 meter = 100 centimeters
1 yard (yd.) = 90 centimeters

Measuring Language

It isn't important whether or not you measure your crazy crochet, unless you plan to make something to wear, or all the parts need to be the same size. Inches, feet, and yards are the usual measuring words, and you already know those.

In other countries the metric measuring system is used. When you buy a ball of yarn made in another country, the paper band will tell you in metric how much it weighs and how much yarn there is. Here are the main metric measurements changed to inches, feet, and yards:

6

Starting, Stopping and Stitches

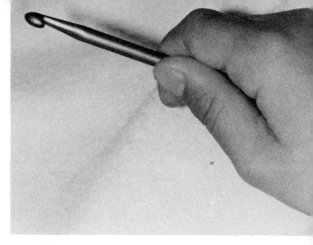

Holding the crochet hook (photo by May Chin)

Holding the crochet hook

Crocheting is easy to do, but it takes a little practice. After you learn to hold the hook and yarn and make the loops at the same time, it will become almost automatic. The kids at University Heights School felt as though they had too many fingers when they first began to learn how to crochet. After a while they got the hang of it and then their fingers flew along. So practice is the answer. The more you do it the easier it is. And that's when the real fun begins.

All crocheting starts with a base. This base is called the "foundation chain." From this base, or foundation, you can then begin to build one row or round on another.

The foundation chain always starts with a slip knot, and from this slip knot you make a chain stitch. From that base of chain stitches, you then build all the other parts.

First things first. Before doing anything else, you must learn how to hold the crochet hook and yarn. Put the crochet hook in your right hand and hold it as though you were holding a shovel. Grasp the hook firmly, but don't press too hard or your fingers will feel cramped and it will be hard to move the crochet hook comfortably. Put the hook down and pick it up a few times. Roll it around in your hand.

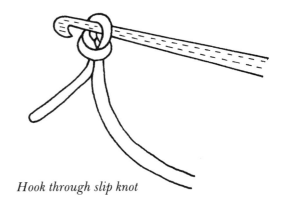

Hook through slip knot

Slip Knot

Now you are ready to make the slip knot. (If you already know how you're a step ahead.) Here's how:

Step 1. Hold the yarn in your left hand four or five inches from the end of the ball.

Step 2. Make a loop with your right hand and hold it in place with the thumb and first finger of your left hand.

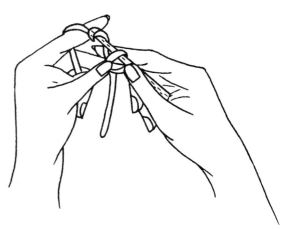

Pulling yarn through slip knot

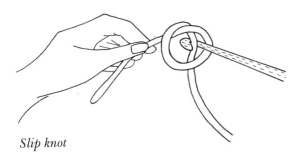

Slip knot

Step 3. Keep the long end of the yarn behind the loop. With the crochet hook pull the yarn through the loop.

Pulling yarn through slip knot (detail)

Step 4. Hold both ends of the yarn together and give them a yank to tighten up the loop on the hook.

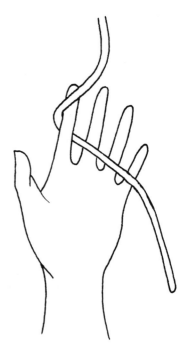

Placing yarn through fingers of left hand

To start crocheting, hold the working yarn this way: close the fingers of your left hand around the yarn and slip your forefinger underneath the yarn up close to the slip knot. The short end of the yarn should come forward and the end attached to the ball in back. Your first finger is the boss in charge of moving the yarn toward the hook as you crochet. It's kind of like a side-step only you are doing it with your fingers.

Take another look at the slip knot drawings to be sure you understand. Are you still confused? Start again and follow each step carefully. Practice making slip knots a few more times. Match your fingers to the drawings.

You're anxious to start crocheting, but unless you learn how to make a slip knot and how to hold the crochet hook and yarn, it won't be any fun.

When I first learned how to crochet a long time ago, my fingers kept getting all tangled up and I felt pretty dumb. After a little more practice, everything began to go right, and then I felt a lot smarter. So even if it all seems like a bunch of gobbledygook in the beginning, crocheting does get easier with practice.

Remember how many times you fell

Gail crocheting at home

Chain Stitch

Okay. Now you know how to make a slip knot. Time to tackle the first stitch of crochet. It's called a chain stitch. The drawings and photos show you how the hook goes underneath the yarn and pulls the yarn through the loop on the hook. Each time the yarn is pulled through the loop it forms a chain stitch.

Step 1. Put the hook into the slip knot

Step 2. Leave the loop on the hook and slide the knot up close to the hook. Put the hook underneath the yarn attached to the ball and catch it with the hook.

Step 3. Pull the yarn through the loop on hook.

off your bike while you were learning to ride? Didn't it seem as though you'd never learn to balance? Then one day, all of a sudden, there you were pedaling away. That's what will happen while you're learning to crochet. Bingo! You've got it.

You have made the first chain stitch.

Repeat steps 2 and 3 to make another chain stitch. Continue this way until you have a big, long chain. One loop grows right into the next one. That wasn't so hard, was it?

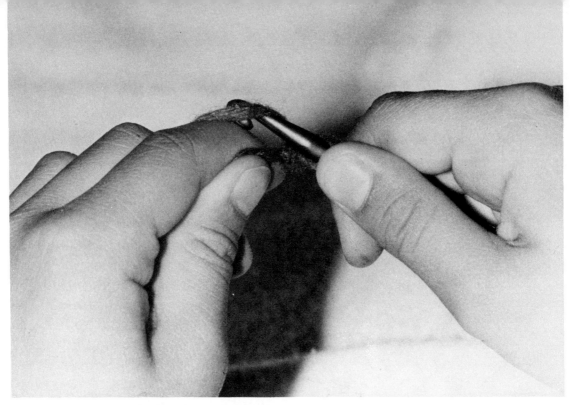

Hook underneath yarn for first chain (photo by
May Chin)

Hook underneath yarn (photo by May Chin)

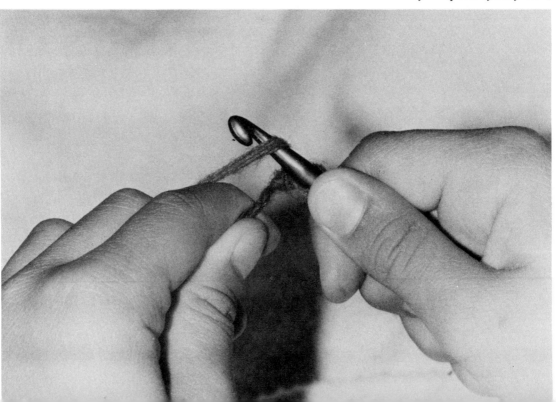

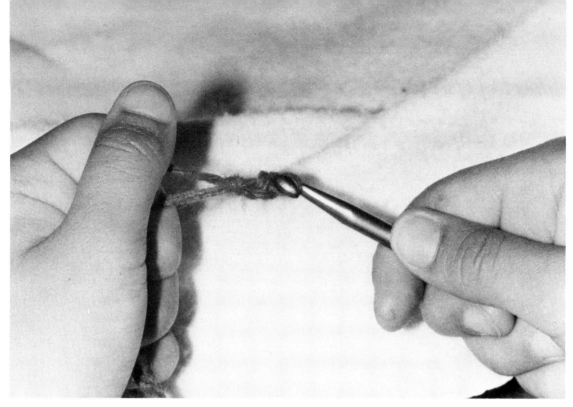

Pulling yarn through loop (photo by May Chin)

Second stitch of chain (photo by May Chin)

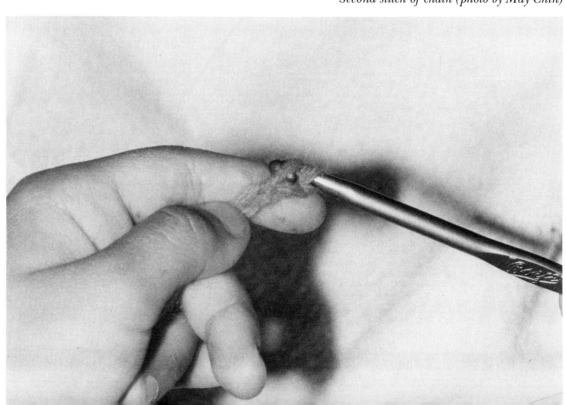

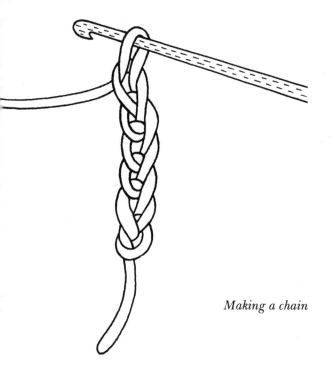

Practice making chain stitches until your fingers work almost without you thinking about them. That's when crocheting starts to get exciting. And remember—always pick up the yarn by moving the hook underneath the yarn from left to right.

Sitting in one place and concentrating hard can make you tired, so it's time to stretch your arms, shake your wrists and jump up and down. Then you'll be all ready to learn some more stitches.

Making a chain

Making a chain (photo by May Chin)

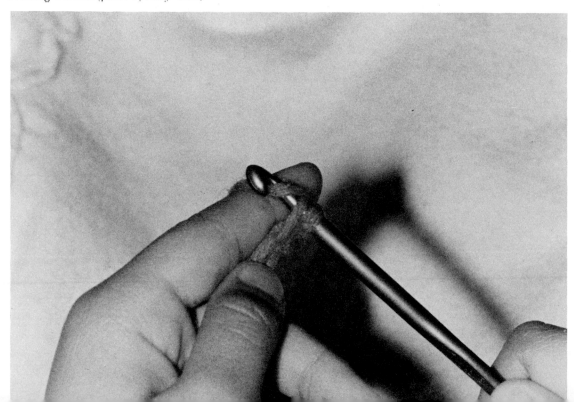

Single Crochet Stitch

Making first single crochet from foundation chain

Step 1. Make a new chain of 20 or 30 stitches, and leave the last loop on the hook.

Step 2. Put the hook under the 2 top threads of the second chain from the hook.

Step 3. Slide the hook underneath the yarn attached to the ball. Pull the yarn through the top threads. There are 2 loops on the hook.

Step 4. Put the hook underneath the yarn again, and pull the yarn through the 2 loops on the hook.

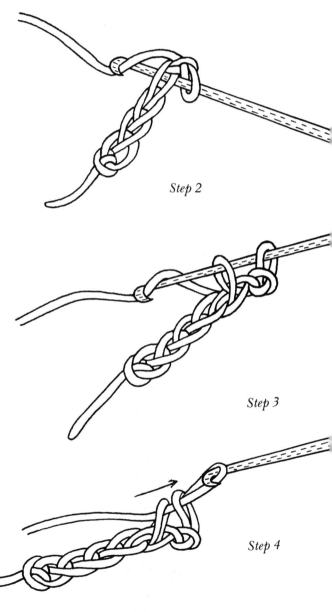

Step 2

Step 3

Step 4

You have made one single crochet stitch and now have one loop on the hook.

Repeat steps 2, 3, and 4 in the next chain stitch, and in every chain stitch until you come to the end of the row. Make one more chain stitch. This is called a *turning stitch*. It helps to keep the edges of your work even when you start the next row. Turn your

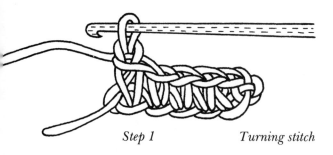

Step 1   *Turning stitch*

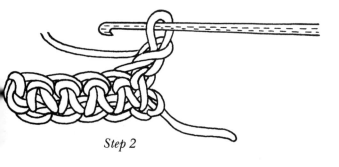

Step 2

and change the shape of your work whenever it suits you. While you are learning all these new things you should know how to do them correctly.

Remember I told you it's like riding a bike? First you learn how to balance and work the pedals at the same time. Then you can go around in circles, up and down curbs, and even ride standing up. Be patient.

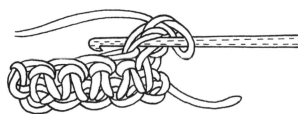

Step 3
Making first stitch in second row of single crochet

work around so that you work from right to left. Make a single crochet stitch in the first stitch next to the turning stitch and in every stitch on that row. Work another turning stitch and complete the next row.

Work back and forth in single crochet. Turn your work around at the end of each row, and remember to make the turning stitch. In a little while you'll be able to recognize the stitches. Later on you can play around

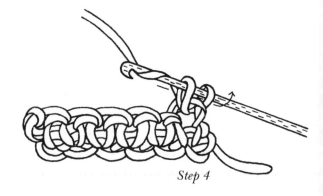

Step 4

Detail of single crochet

Sometimes concentrating so hard makes you grab the hook and yarn too firmly. You'll find yourself scowling, too. This can tire you. When you feel yourself scrunching up and grabbing the hook and yarn really tight, stop for a while and go do something else.

Double Crochet Stitch

The double crochet stitch is taller than the single crochet stitch, so you'll be using a little more yarn. The double crochet stitch is about equal to two rows, so it will make your material grow faster. Here's how:

Step 1. Make another 20- or 30-stitch chain.

Step 2. Wrap the yarn around the hook once (this is called a "yarn over"). Put the hook into the *4th* chain from the hook.

Step 3. Catch the yarn and pull it through the chain stitch (there are 3 loops on the hook).

Step 4. Put the hook underneath the yarn again, and pull the yarn through *2* loops on the hook.

Step 5. Put the hook underneath the yarn once more and pull the yarn through the remaining 2 loops on the hook.

That's one double crochet.

Repeat steps 2, 3, 4, and 5 in every chain stitch all across the row. Now you are ready to turn around and double crochet the next row. To turn the row make 3 chain stitches. The three chains count as the turning stitches and are equal in height to 1 double crochet stitch.

Double crochet in foundation chain

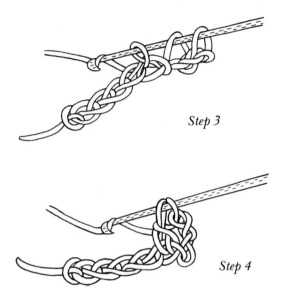

Step 3

Step 4

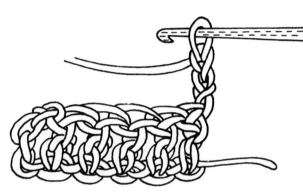

3 turning chains for double crochet

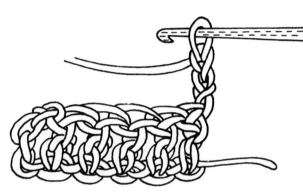

Step 5

Turn your work around so that the row you've just completed is on top. Double crochet in every stitch on that row. Crochet back and forth this way, remembering the 3 turning chains. Can you tell the difference between a single crochet stitch and a double crochet stitch?

Now you know how to make a slip knot, a chain stitch, a single crochet stitch, and a double crochet stitch.

Let's put them all together.

Start with the slip knot and make a chain—about 25 stitches. You don't have to count exactly, just as long as the chain is long enough for a good sample. Work a few rows of single crochet on top of the beginning chain. (Check the directions for a single crochet in case you've forgotten.) Don't forget the turning stitch.

Single crochet back and forth for a few rows. Continuing on the same sample, make a few rows of double crochet. Go back and work some more single crochet and see if you can tell where single crochet changes to double crochet.

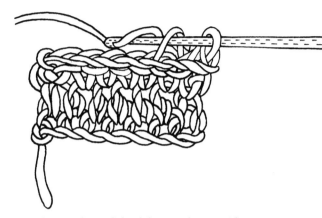

Crocheting through back loop to form a ridge— single crochet

Ribbed Single and Double Crochet

Here's how to change the look of single and double crochet stitches just by putting the hook through the back thread of a stitch. When you put the hook through both threads of a stitch, your material has a flat appearance. You can change that by putting the hook through the back thread of a stitch. It makes a ridge on the side facing you.

Try it first with the single crochet stitch. See how it forms a ridge? Do a few rows on your practice piece until you can recognize the change.

Work a few rows of double crochet stitch in the back of the stitch. Remember to make the 3 turning chain stitches at the end of each row.

Go one step further. This time put the hook through the thread closest to you, and do this in every stitch in the row. The ridge is now on the back side of the material. It's just opposite. Make ridges front or back; it doesn't matter. Crochet some ridges on the side facing you, then make some on the other side.

Crocheting through back loop to form a ridge—double crochet

Cup and saucer with single crochet ridges

Practice making single and double crochet ridges for a while. Then try all the stitches with other kinds of yarn and a larger or smaller hook. Your material will look different each time you change yarns and hook.

There is lots more to learn about crocheting, so you'd better take a break and rest your hands and eyes for a while.

Ridged single crochet

7

Making Your Work Fatter and Skinnier

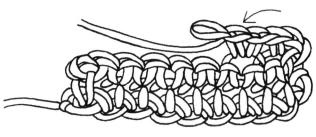

Single crochet increase

When you want to make your work fatter, *increase* the number of stitches. To make it skinnier *decrease* the number of stitches. It's sort of like going on a diet. You can increase or decrease stitches anywhere you want—at the beginning or end of a row, in the middle, or anywhere else.

Increasing

It's a snap to increase because all you do is make two stitches in the same stitch. Each time a stitch is added your work becomes a little wider. Increasing a stitch in *every* stitch will make a ruffle. Increase only at the beginning and end of a row and your work will grow at an angle. Because this is crazy

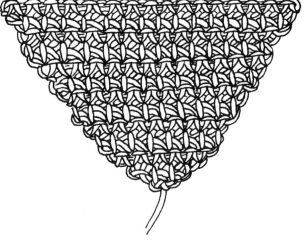

Increase at beginning and end of rows

crochet, you can increase stitches as often as you feel like it. But if you make something to wear, you must be more careful and increase in exactly the right place.

On your practice piece, work in single crochet and increase 1 stitch in the first stitch. Work even across the row until you come to the last stitch. Increase in that stitch. You have added two stitches. Make a turning stitch, then increase in the first and last stitch of that row. Work back and forth for a few rows, increasing in the first and last stitch of each row. Your work is quickly getting wider. Increase less rapidly by increasing in the first and last stitch of *every other* row.

On the same sample increase in every *other* stitch. Now you've made a ruffle. Work some more rows this way and watch what happens to the ruffle. On the next row increase in *every* stitch. See what a fat ruffle you've made?

Make some increases wherever you want to and watch the material change again.

Decreasing

Your work will become skinnier when you decrease stitches. It's just the opposite of increasing. To decrease in crochet you make *one* stitch from two.

Ballerina with ruffled Tutu—single crocheted with knitting worsted

Single crochet decrease—beginning of row

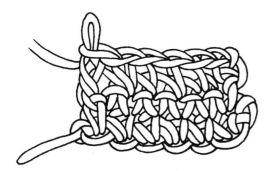

Single crochet decrease—end of row

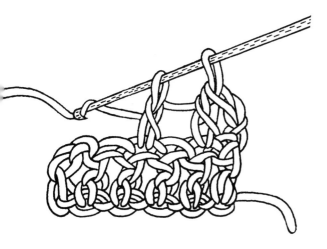

Double crochet decrease

Each time you subtract a stitch your work becomes narrower.

Use the same sample. On the next row, put the hook into the second stitch from the hook. Make a single crochet. Work all the stitches on that row until you come to the last 2 stitches. *Skip* 1 stitch and make a single crochet in the last stitch. You have subtracted 2 stitches. Turn your work around and decrease 1 stitch at the beginning and end of that row. Work back and forth decreasing one stitch at the beginning and end of each row until there are about 4 stitches left. Your work has become narrower (it looks like a triangle), just by skipping those first and last stitches.

Decrease less rapidly by decreasing only at the beginning and end of every *other* row.

Make another chain and work even for a few rows, then decrease stitches anywhere you please. Pretty soon you'll be able to decide where and when you want to make your work skinnier. Page 38 shows two pitchers. First the bases were made for the bottom, then a few stitches were decreased on each round until there

Stair Step Increasing and Decreasing

were just a few stitches for the neck of the pitchers. Stitches were then added to form the spout.

Increase and decrease on your sample until you feel in control of the stitches.

There's still another way to increase or decrease stitches. I call it "Stair stepping," because that's what it looks like. You add or subtract the stitches at the beginning or end of a row with this method.

This is stair step increasing: Chain 15 stitches then single crochet back and forth for a few rows. Crochet across the next row. At the end of that row make 4 chains. Turn your work around and single crochet in the second chain from the hook. Finish the row. Work even for 3 more rows. At

Two crocheted pitchers made with knitting worsted

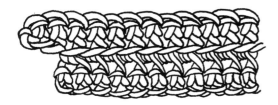

Stair step increase

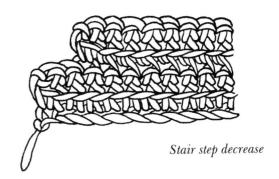

Stair step decrease

the end of the third row, add 4 more chains. Repeat the above directions. Be sure to add the extra chains at the same edge every time.

You can add as many chains as you please—whatever works with your designs. Work any number of rows between the added chains.

Stair step decreasing is opposite from "stair step" increasing. Make reverse "stair steps" by stopping before you come to the end of the row. Try it.

Make a foundation chain and crochet 2 or 3 rows. Work across the next row but stop about 3 stitches before the end of the row. Make a turning chain stitch and work back on those stitches. Crochet 2 more rows, but stop 3 stitches before you reach the end of the second row. Make a turning stitch and work back. The idea is the same as "stair step" increasing only reversed.

Turn your work upside-down and it looks like the increasing method.

Stair stepping can work up into a whole lot of interesting shapes. Start by making some stair step increases, and on the same sample, change to the decreasing method. Turn your sample on its side and it will look like an evergreen tree. Turn it on its head and you'll have a nutty looking "V." Make some stairs one size and some another size. The rest is up to you.

Here are some other ways to make your work skinnier or fatter. Start with a larger crochet hook and use the same yarn. The larger hook makes fatter stitches. Change to a smaller hook and your work will be skinnier.

Use a skinny yarn for a few rows, then change to a big, fat, puffy yarn, but don't change the size of the crochet hook. The part you crocheted

Sample of different kinds of yarn single crocheted with one size hook

that's the whole idea of crazy crochet, and they'll be your own invention!

It's all right to start from scratch if you're still not too sure of yourself. You don't have to worry about how much yarn or string you'll need, because anything goes.

You're the boss of the hook and yarn and you can tell them what to do. If you like what happens maybe your practice work will turn into an interesting wall hanging.

Here's a little trick that might help you remember each new thing—write it down on a little piece of paper and pin it to your sample. For instance, when you do a double crochet stitch, make a note of it. If you forget, look at the sample again.

with the fat yarn will be wider than the part you crocheted with the skinny yarn.

Since you're only practicing, play around with different kinds of yarns and sizes of hooks, increasing and decreasing wherever you want to. You'll make some really nutty shapes, but

8

Joining New Yarn

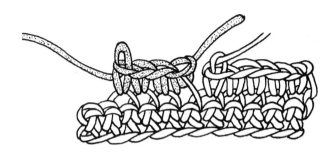

Starting new yarn

Have you been wondering how to start a new ball of yarn when the old one is all used up, or when you want to change colors in the middle of your creation? It happens to all crocheters, and here's how:

Sometimes you'll run out of yarn in the middle of a row, sometimes you'll be lucky and run out at the end. If you were crocheting something to wear, it would look a little better to start the new yarn at the beginning of a row. For this crazy kind of crochet it doesn't matter.

Leave a little tail of the old yarn, and about the same amount of the new yarn. Start right in crocheting. Crochet 2 or 3 rows, or rounds, whatever you happen to be doing, then go back and tie the loose ends in a knot so they won't come loose. Later on, weave the dangling ends right back into the material with your crochet hook. Leave the loose ends hanging if you want to.

Start a new color the same way. If you want the new color to start in a special place, better plan ahead. Leave a little longer tail just in case you change your mind and things don't work out.

9
Fastening Off

10
Some Special Shapes

When you want to end your project, and are all through crocheting, you "fasten off" the yarn. Do it this way:

Finish the row or round you are working, then make one more chain stitch and pull it up into a great big loop (about three inches long). Cut the yarn attached to the ball and pull the cut end through the big loop. Be sure to pull the yarn good and tight so your work won't unravel. Weave the cut end of the yarn back through the material. Or just leave it.

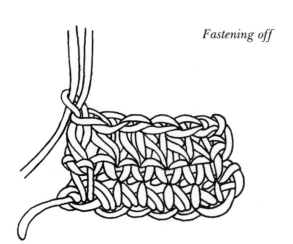

Fastening off

All kinds of shapes are possible with crazy crochet. Besides working back and forth, you can go around in circles, turn corners, work in angles, and any other shape you can think of. Try the ones described in this chapter then design something yourself, using any one, or all of them.

Square

All four sides of a square should measure the same. To begin, crochet a chain about 4 inches long. Work back and forth in single crochet (don't forget the turning stitch), until the top and bottom measure the same as the left and right sides. Start another square, only this time work in double crochet (3 turning chains). Double crochet is about twice as high as single

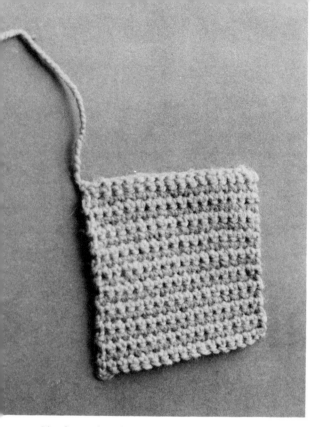

Single crocheted square

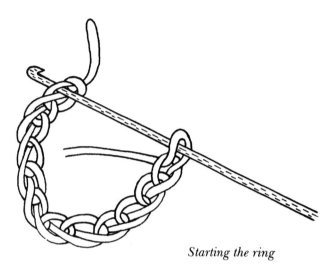

Starting the ring

crochet so you'll need only about half the number of rows.

Rings

Join both ends of a chain and you'll have a ring. Make a whole bunch of chains and rings. This is how:

Start with a slip knot and make a 20- or 30-stitch chain. Count back 10 chain stitches and put the hook into that tenth stitch and make a slip stitch. You have made one ring. Add some

Connecting two ends of the chain

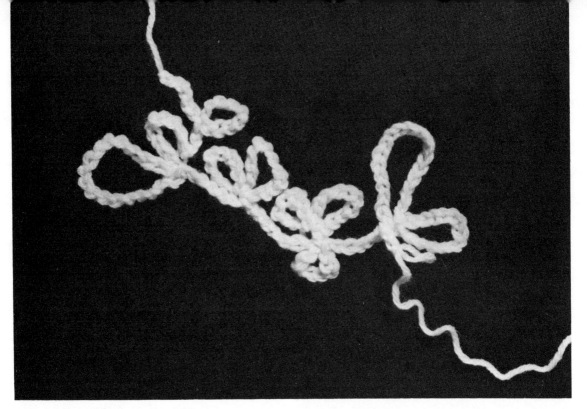

Connected rings and chains

Detail

more chain stitches then make another slip stitch in the same stitch as the first one. At left are lots of chains and rings all connected together. Invent your own pattern of chains and rings. The rings don't have to be the same size. For smaller rings use fewer chain stitches. For larger rings, make more chain stitches.

Starting the circle

Circles

Join both ends of a short chain to start a circle. Start with a slip knot and chain 6 or 7 stitches. Put the hook back into the first stitch of the chain and make a slip stitch. Work 2 single crochet stitches (increases) in *every* chain stitch until you come back to the starting chain. Attach a yarn marker right there to remind you where to begin the new round. When you crochet circles each row is called a "round." On this round increase in every *other* stitch. Increase every *other* stitch on *every other* round and you will end up with a big circle. Change colors or the size of the crochet hook and notice the difference in your circles.

You can make a stack of pancakes with circles, or the bottom of a glass,

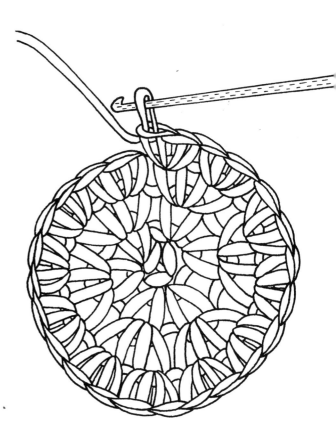

Increasing the circle

*Mr. Crab with 8 claws—made from two circles,
stuffed and crocheted together, tiny white circles
for eyes, single crocheted claws. Made by Kathy*

Side view

Bottom

or a pillow. Dream up some other ways to use circles.

Triangles

There are two ways to make a triangle: start at the point of the triangle or start at the bottom.

To start at the point, make a slip knot and 1 chain stitch. Turn your work and increase 1 stitch at the beginning and end of each row until the triangle is as wide as you want it to be. Fasten off.

Triangle starting from point

Triangle starting from base

Diamond shape

Start at the base and you'll be working backwards. Chain 15, then decrease at the beginning and end of each row, until there are two loops on the hook. Fasten off.

For a triangle with a more gradual slope, increase or decrease only every *other* row.

Diamonds

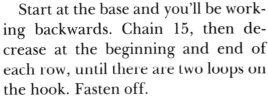

The diamond shape is made by starting with a triangle using the *increasing* method then immediately reverse it by *decreasing*.

Use a single crochet or double crochet stitch for your triangles. Experiment with other yarns and different sizes of hooks.

Ovals

Footballs, race tracks, kitchen tables, eggs—all of these have oval shapes. You can crochet an oval, too. Instead of crocheting back and forth you'll be going up one side and down the next. At each end you must add extra stitches in order to turn the corner.

Chain 6 stitches. Make a single crochet in each chain stitch. Instead of turning your work as you do to make a square, work 3 single crochet stitches in the last stitch. Continue to single crochet down the other side until you reach the last stitch. (You'd better put a marker here.) Make 3 single crochets in that last stitch. Continue around, and at each end be sure to work 3 single crochets in one stitch to turn the corner. Make some double crochet ovals, too.

You may have to add a stitch at each end so the oval will stay nice and flat. If you don't care, maybe you'll get a hump in the middle, or have a lopsided oval. You might even like those better, and who cares, anyway?

Half-Ovals

Would you like to crochet just half an oval? Instead of going up one side and down the other, half-ovals are crocheted back and forth—just like squares or oblongs, except you increase stitches about every other row.

Start with a 14-stitch chain. Work 1 row even in single crochet. On the next row increase 1 stitch in the *first* stitch and in every *third* stitch across the row. End with an increase in the

Oval shape

Half-oval—single crochet

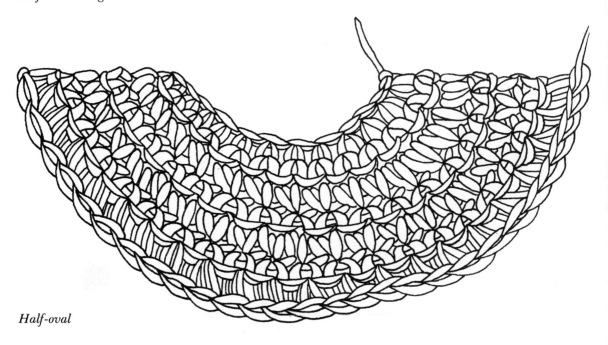

Half-oval

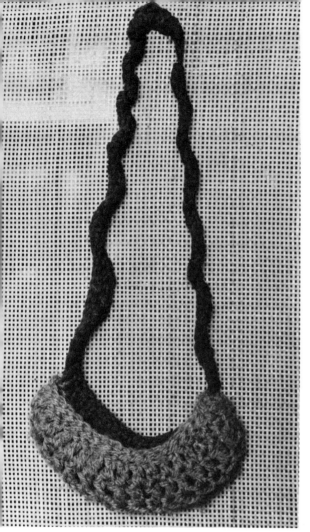

Shoulder bag—half-oval. Single and double crochet, with double chain shoulder strap. Made by University Heights student

Now that you know how to make the half-ovals, see if you can create some interesting ways to use them. Make some in flat yarns and some in bumpy yarns and arrange them any way you please. Sew a bunch of them together and hang them on the wall.

Oblongs

Oblongs are simply squares that look as though they've been stretched out. They are longer than they are wide, and you can use a single or double crochet to make these, too. Chain about 20 stitches, then work back and forth until your work measures up and down about half the width of the chain. That's all there is to it.

last stitch. Repeat these two rows until the arc is as large as you want.

For a more gentle half-oval, increase only every fourth stitch every other row. There is no hard and fast rule because you are the designer.

Oblong shape

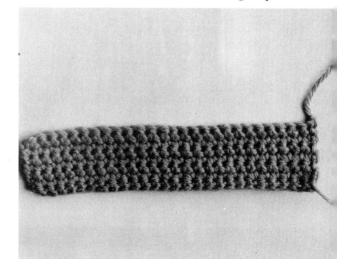

Tunnels and Tubes

When you get tired of crocheting back and forth, connect your chain to make a ring, and then crochet round and round. Before you know it you'll have a tunnel or a tube.

To start, chain about 20 stitches. Put the crochet hook back into the beginning stitch of the chain and pull the yarn through both loops. You've connected both ends of the chain and have one loop on the hook.

Crocheted tunnel

Put the hook through the next stitch in the chain and pull the yarn through. Now you have two loops on the hook. Once more pull the yarn through both loops on the hook. You have made a single crochet stitch. Single crochet in every stitch, working round and round, without increasing or decreasing stitches. In other words "working even." After crocheting a few rounds you'll be able to see how the tunnel or tube is formed. Make it as long as you want. When you are tired of going round and round, fasten off. Get the idea? Do you feel a bit clumsy? You'd better practice awhile more.

Tubes and tunnels can be used in a variety of ways. They can be buildings, or people, or trees, or even animals.

Start with fewer stitches for a skinnier tunnel. More stitches for a fatter tunnel. Make a goofy-shaped tunnel with bulges along the way. You do this by increasing for a few rounds and then decreasing. Increase and decrease on only one part of a round—you'll have a lopsided tunnel. Who cares?

Crochet some tall, skinny tunnels or some short, fat ones. Place a marker at the end of the first round to remind you when to start the next one.

Make a bunch of tunnels, all different sizes, shapes and colors. Invent some interesting ways to display them.

All the shapes described in this chapter should give you a pretty good idea of what you can do with your crochet hook. Try them all, then create something new. Close your eyes and think of a shape, then try to crochet that shape just the way you saw it in your head. This ought to keep you busy for a while.

11

Finger Crocheting

You don't have a crochet hook? Use your fingers! To finger crochet your forefinger takes the place of the crochet hook and the result looks exactly the same as if you'd used a hook.

So just imagine that your first finger is a big crochet hook. In the beginning, for this experiment, work with a fatter yarn because it's much easier to hook your finger around it. You can make chains and single and double crochet stitches. Like this:

Chains

Step 1. Make a slip knot.

Step 2. Put your forefinger through the slip knot loop.

Step 3. Leave the loop on your finger and catch the yarn attached

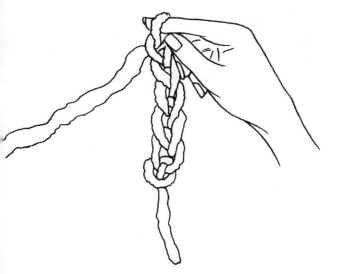

to the ball with the end of your finger. Pull it through the loop. (Your thumb might have to help you out in case the yarn tries to slip away from your finger.)

You have made the first chain stitch. Repeat steps 2 and 3 until you can do them easily.

Finger crocheting chain stitch

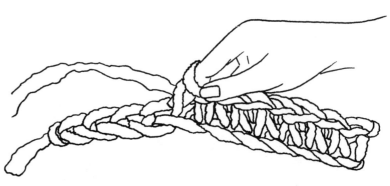

Finger crocheting single crochet

Single Finger Crocheting

Single finger crocheting is almost like working with the crochet hook except your first finger has to wiggle a little more.

Step 1. Start a new chain and make about 10 chain stitches.

Step 2. Leave the loop on your finger. Put your finger through the first chain stitch next to your finger.

Step 3. Catch the yarn with your finger.

Step 4. Pull the yarn through the chain stitch. There are two loops on your finger.

Step 6. Put your finger underneath the yarn again and pull the yarn through both loops on your finger. There! You've made one single crochet stitch.

Repeat steps 2 through 6 in each chain stitch on that row. Make a turning stitch at the end of the row. Turn your work around so that you work from right to left and repeat all the steps for single crochet. Work a few more rows. Your material looks as though you used a crochet hook, doesn't it? Well, that's our secret.

Double Finger Crocheting

Now let's see if you can do some double finger crochet. Go back to page 30 and follow all the steps for double crochet. Whenever the instructions tell you to "put the crochet hook through," substitute "finger" for "crochet hook" and that's all there is to it!

Make it easier on yourself and have someone read you each step of the instructions while your fingers do the work.

Practice double finger crocheting for a while, then switch back to single crocheting.

Making Shapes

Make some rings, circles, ovals and squares using only your fingers. Get the idea? All you have to keep in mind is that finger crocheting is the same as regular crocheting, but without the

Finger crocheted fat yarn

Finger crocheted skinny stuff

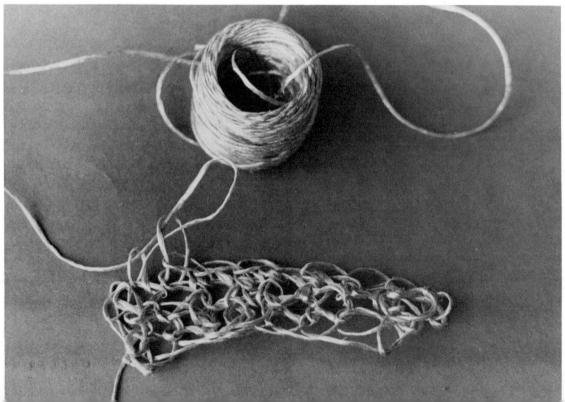

hook. You can make all the shapes you've already learned, and any others you invent.

Try finger crocheting with other kinds of yarns. Some skinny, some fat. Your finger is about the same size as a great big crochet hook, so the fatter yarn makes firmer stitches. The skinnier yarn makes looser stitches. The sample top left was made with a thick wool yarn. The sample in bottom left was made with plastic twine. See how different they are? The plastic yarn is pretty skinny so the result is lacy and open.

Finger crochet your newspaper. Spread a sheet of newspaper on the table and cut it into ½-inch diagonal strips. Paste the end of one strip to the end of another so you have a continuous strip. Let the paste dry thoroughly. Now finger crochet the paper strips.

Handle the paper a little more care-

Cutting newspaper for finger crocheting

fully than regular yarn to avoid tearing it. The printing makes some interesting designs.

If you decide you like to crochet with paper, you can buy a roll of unprinted paper called "newsprint." Go to the newspaper office in your city and ask if they'll sell you some. Sometimes there are roll ends they might give you.

Be sure to wash your hands with soap after you finish crocheting printed newspaper because the black ink comes off on your hands.

12

Found Stuff

Pretty rocks you find on the beach, discarded jewelry, a piece of driftwood, buttons, beads, scraps of fur, an interesting piece of metal, are just a few examples of stuff that might add some interest. This is called "found stuff."

Raid your mother's sewing box for odd buttons. How about some big, fat beads with great big holes in them? These are all useful.

The kids at University Heights School used a lot of junk jewelry. You can sew an old string of beads right on to the surface of your crocheting. Lay your material on a flat surface and arrange the beads on the material. Wiggle them around in a pleasing pattern. Thread your sewing needle with matching thread and sew the necklace to the surface with an overcast stitch (Page 70).

Or add some beads right into a crocheted necklace. See Page 64 for directions.

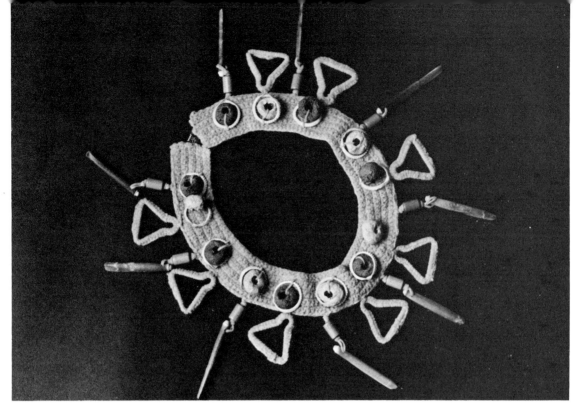

Neckpiece with found objects. Single crochet—clay beads, shells, wooden beads, bones, suspender holders

Some found stuff—cork coaster with big holes, metal bells, big wooden beads, coral, clay beads, pinecones, driftwood, broken sand dollar, big rock

Keep an eye out for some unusual things to use as hangers for your crazy crochet project, such as a coat hanger, or a smooth branch, or a piece of chain. As you work along other ideas will occur to you.

13
Correcting Mistakes

14
The Razzle Dazzles

Although there really aren't any mistakes in crazy crochet, there might be a time when you've made too many stitches for your design, or your material is longer than you planned, or you have increased when you meant to decrease, or the other way around. You don't have to correct them—just think of another design. But if you really think they should be corrected, it's very easy to do. Take the crochet hook out of the loop and unravel the stitches back to the right place. Put the hook back into the loop and go on with your project.

That's what's so terrific about crochet—it's easy to undo and rework. Sometimes it's just as much fun to rip as it is to crochet!

Want to have some more fun now that you know how to make all those crazy shapes? Add some color. Or add lots of colors. You can start a new color at the beginning or end of a row, or partway across. You can crochet with one color until it's all used up, then start the new color wherever the old one ends.

Everything in the whole world has some color. It's all around you. Color can make you laugh out loud, or it can give you a case of the blues. Take a walk in your neighborhood and look at all the different colors of houses. Notice how Mother Nature puts colors together. She mixes them all up and they all seem to fit. After a heavy rain, nature's colors seem to sparkle.

For more ideas on how to use color, go to the library and look at some art

Crocheted chains crawling all over wire hanger

books, or poke around at an art gallery. Artists use color in exciting ways.

To help you make up your mind, make a color sampler of your own.

Get a big sheet of paper and mark off some lines about one inch apart. With colored chalk or marking pens, use a different color between each set of lines. When you see the colors all together on that big sheet of paper, you'll soon begin to plan how best to use color in your crochet. After you find the right combination for your project, take the color samples to a yarn store and try to match them. Or maybe there's some yarn at home that will work.

Making a color chart

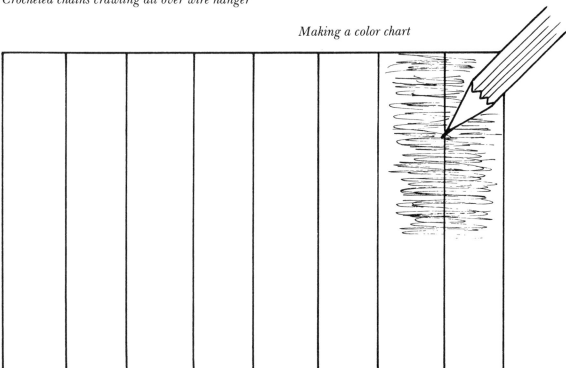

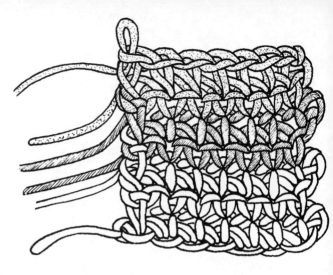

Crocheting stripes—single crochet

Rainbows

Are you ready to experiment now? Crochet a few rows of one color. At the beginning of the next row drop the old color and cut the yarn, leaving about a 3- or 4-inch tail. Leave about the same length and start crocheting with the new color. Work a few rows. Start another color the same way.

Start a new color in the middle of a row the same way, only this time the cut ends will be in the middle instead of at the end. The cut ends of the yarn can be all on the same side, both sides, or at each end. Be sure to go back and tie the cut ends in a knot so they don't unravel, then weave them back into the material. Or you can leave all the tails hanging.

Stripes

Choose a color and start your striping experiment with the basic chain. The chain can be any length. Work 1 row in single crochet. The beginning chain and the first row will count as 2 rows. Make a turning chain in the same color, and start the new color with a single crochet stitch in the first stitch of the last row. Continue with the new color, working a single crochet in each stitch. Make another turning chain and work 1 more row in the new color. There are two rows of each color. Always make the turning stitch in the old color, before changing to the new one.

Each time you start a new color, there will be a little tail of yarn. The stripes can be as wide or as narrow as will fit your design. With even-numbered rows of stripes all the cut ends will be on the same side of your work. On odd-numbered rows the cut ends will be on both sides. Try some stripes of one row and combine them with wider three-row stripes, or any other number of rows. The new color can be joined at either end of your work. It doesn't matter. Get the picture? The stripes can all be worked from the same kind of yarn. Combine a flat yarn of one color with a bumpy one of a different color. Gather up all your odds and ends for a test pattern.

You can stripe your tunnels and tubes, too. When you are bored working back and forth, switch to them. Can't remember how to start the tunnel? Go back to page 52 to refresh your memory. The striped tunnel is crocheted exactly like a regular tunnel, except you will be changing colors every couple of rounds, or even every three or four rounds.

Striped tunnel

Crochet all around the edge of your sample in one color, then start another color for the next row. Stripes can go back and forth or all catywampus.

The example above was made with scraps of knitting worsted. Each stripe is two rounds high.

The two Chris kids crocheting stripes

15

Inserting Beads and Other Things

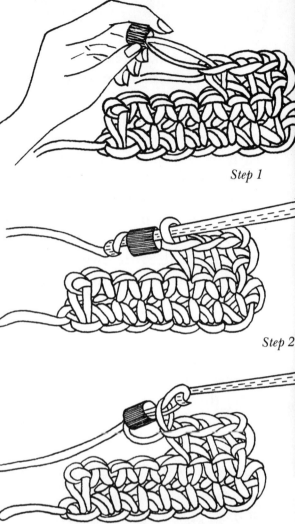

Step 1

Decorate your crocheting with beads or objects that have big holes in them. The hole should be large enough to slip the crochet hook through the hole easily.

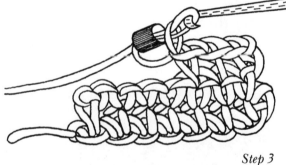

Step 2

Earlier we talked about all the stuff you can work into your masterpiece, such as beads, junk jewelry, stones. If you can find a bunch of beads with big holes you are ready for the next step.

Crochet a few rows so you'll have a solid background to work on.

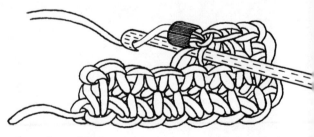

Step 3

Step 1. Hold the bead in your left hand, slip the loop off the crochet hook and stretch it out.

Step 2. Slide the hook through the hole in the bead and catch the stretched-out loop.

Inserting a bead

Step 4

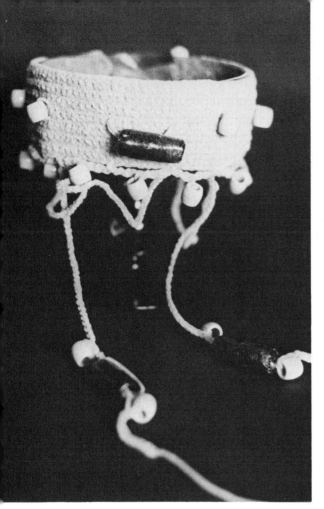

Neckpiece. Single crochet and chains with wooden beads and glass beads crocheted into material

Practice inserting stuff until you have it down pat. To help you along the way, have someone read each step as you work with the crochet hook.

Sometimes the bead doesn't have a hole big enough for the yarn to slide through. Sew it on later with a needle and thread. Remember, there is more than one way to solve a problem.

There are lots of other neat kinds of junk stuff I haven't even mentioned. Garage sales and thrift stores are gold mines. How about trading stuff with a friend?

Neckpiece—detail

Step 3. Pull the loop through the hole in the bead. Immediately make a single crochet in the next stitch. You've just crocheted the bead directly into your material.

Crochet a few more stitches and repeat the above steps. Continue to add beads whenever you like. Add other objects with holes in the same way.

16

Don't Throw Anything Away

Some yarns may be pretty expensive, so don't spend any more money than you have to. Recycling is one way to save money. Check around for an old crocheted hat or scarf. Rip it all out, wash the yarn (if it needs washing) and use the yarn for your crazy crochet. When you unravel the yarn it will be all crinkly and wiggly. It doesn't matter. Use it just like that with all the kinks, and the texture will be interesting when you crochet with it. First wind it back into a ball. It will be easier to work with.

Wash the yarn before using it over again, and it will be just like new. Here's how: get a big sheet of cardboard, or a large hardcover book. As you unravel, wind the yarn around the book. Tie a piece of string around

the wound yarn in a couple of places, then slip it off the board or book.

Add a little bit of liquid soap to a sinkful of cool or lukewarm water. Squish the yarn around a few times. Squeeze out the extra water. Do *not* twist the yarn. Rinse it three or four times in clear, lukewarm water until all the soap is removed. If you can't tell, maybe an adult will help you. Roll the washed yarn in a clean bath towel. Press it with your hands until most of the extra water is soaked up by the towel. See how the kinks have disappeared?

Hang the yarn over the bathtub faucet to dry. This could take a few hours, so every once in a while check it out. If the yarn still feels soggy, give it a squeeze, and turn the yarn around so the air can get to it. After the yarn is completely dry, put it back on the cardboard or the book, and rewind it into a ball. You're ready to start a new creation.

It's a big "NO-NO" to ever put your washed yarn in the dryer, just to hurry the drying time. You'd have a real mess on your hands.

So don't throw any yarn away just because it's old. You can reuse it lots of times and make something different each time.

17

Connecting the Parts

By now you must have a whole pile of shapes you've been experimenting with and are wondering how to put the pieces together. You can connect them with a slip stitch, a single or double crochet stitch, or sew the parts together.

You'll need your big-eyed yarn needle and T-pins, and, of course, your crochet hook.

Before joining one part to another, lay the parts on a flat surface (the table or the floor). Put them side by side, or one below the other, or angle them, until you are satisfied. Pin one to another with the T-pins. Don't fret if the pieces aren't exactly the same size. You can wiggle them to fit by adjusting the pins. Start pinning from each end toward the middle. If they still don't look right, wiggle them some more.

Pinning the pieces together

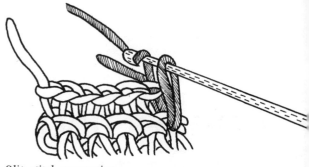

Slip stitch connection

Crochet Connections

First, let's connect the parts with your crochet hook. There are three ways to do this—a slip stitch, single crochet or double crochet. The slip stitch makes a flat joining and is hardly noticeable —unless you use a different color on purpose. The single and double crochet connections form a stand-up ridge that can turn into an interesting decoration.

Slip Stitch Connection

Pin the pieces together. Leave a 3- or 4-inch length of yarn, and put the crochet hook through the top loops of both pieces *at the same time*. Pull the yarn through both sets of loops. There is 1 loop on the crochet hook. Put the hook through the next top loops of both pieces, catch the yarn, pull it through both loops and *through the loop on the hook at the same time*. You have made the first connection with a slip stitch.

Continue this way all along the pinned edges. Don't pull the slip stitches too tight—they should stretch with your material, otherwise the seam might pop.

When you come to the end and have made the last slip stitch, cut the yarn about 4 inches from the hook and pull the cut end through the loop on the hook (page 42). You have connected the two parts and locked the yarn so it won't unravel.

Single Crochet Connection

Pin 2 parts together as you did for the slip stitch connection. Slide the hook into the top loops of *both sections* and make a single crochet stitch. Single crochet in each set of stitches on the pinned edges. Fasten off. See the stand-up ridge? This connection is bulkier than the slip stitch. It adds

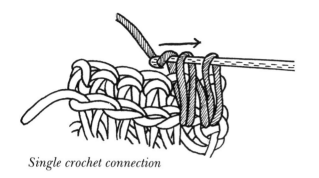

Single crochet connection

texture to your design. It also draws attention to the connection. You'll use a little more yarn, too.

Single crochet connection with squares going in opposite direction

Double Crochet Connection

The double crochet connection is worked exactly like the single crochet connection, except the double crochet forms a taller ridge, and you'll use about twice as much yarn. Jazz up your design with this connection. Use more than one color, if you like the idea. Better plan ahead if you decide on this one.

The Sewing Connection

An overcast stitch made with your big-eyed yarn needle and a separate piece of yarn is an easy way to connect the parts. Here's how:

Again, pin the pieces together the way you want them. Measure off a length of yarn—about 14 or 16 inches long, depending how long a seam you have. For example, for a 7-inch seam, a 16-inch length of yarn should be plenty. Don't be too stingy. Add an extra inch or two, just to be sure.

Double Crochet Connection

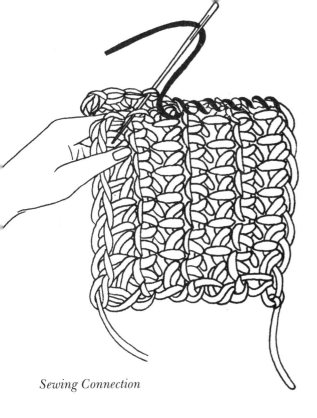

Sewing Connection

both pieces at once, from back to front. Do this once more to anchor the first stitch. Put the needle through over the top from back to front. Continue the same way all along the edge. At the end, make one or two more overcast stitches on top of the last one. Leave a couple of inches of yarn, and cut. Weave any loose ends back into the material after all the parts have been sewn together.

Thread the needle with the cut yarn. If you have trouble getting the cut end of the yarn through the eye of the needle, wet the end, and twist it with your fingers. The yarn should slide through easily. Here's another little trick if you still have trouble—put a tiny drop of clear nail polish on the cut end. Let it dry, then slip that end through the eye of the needle.

To overcast, work from right to left if you are right-handed, and from left to right if you are left-handed. Hold the pinned material firmly in one hand; leave a little tail. Starting at the right edge, put the needle through

Think Before You Start

Before you start to connect all the parts, think about how you want your creation to look when it's all done. Do you want the joinings to be part of the decoration? Would you rather they didn't show? You should make up your mind ahead of time, so it's wise to try all the ways of connecting the parts before you begin.

Maybe you'd like to connect some parts with a slip stitch and others by sewing them together. That's OK, too. Then you can begin to plan how to decorate your masterpiece.

18

Decorations

Decorating crazy crochet is the most fun of all—you can really let your imagination zing.

Make some tassels or fringes. They're both easy and fun. Add some fringe along the edges, up the sides, or anywhere else you can think of. Crochet a single or double crochet stitch in a contrasting color all around the edges, then add beads and other stuff. If these don't appeal to you, invent some decorations of your own.

Tassels

Cut some cardboard about 4 inches long and 3 inches wide. Wrap the yarn around the cardboard until you have a big bundle. Cut another length of yarn about 5 inches long. Slide this piece under the yarn on the cardboard and up to one end. Tie the two ends together in a good, firm knot.

Cut the bundle of yarn at the other end. Snip off another 5-inch piece of yarn. Wind it around the whole bundle about an inch or so below the first tie. Tie a good tight knot. Trim any scraggly ends with your embroidery scissors.

Make the tassels all the same color or all different colors. Make a whole

Making a tassel

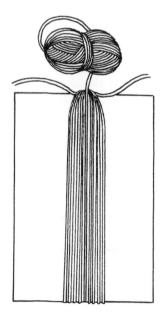

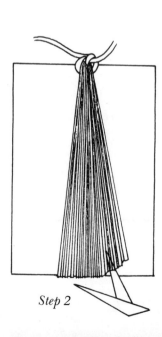

Step 1　　　　　*Step 2*　　　　　*Step 3*

row of them right down the middle of your work. Cut a bigger piece of cardboard and make some giant tassels. Attach them to a big stick and be a cheerleader. Can you think of other ways to decorate with tassels?

Fringes

Make a border of fringe on a wall hanging. Decorate a sweater, or cover a whole crocheted hat with fringe. Combine two or more colors in one fringe. Combine different kinds of yarn, too.

Use the same cardboard you used for tassels. Scotch tape the cut end of the yarn to one end of the cardboard and wrap the yarn around it. Each time you wrap the yarn it counts as one strand of fringe. For instance, for a 2-strand fringe, wrap the yarn around the board 2 times. Wrap the yarn 8 times for four 2-strand fringes. For four 3-strand fringes, wrap the yarn 12 times.

The fringes don't have to match if you don't want them to. Make some fat ones and skinny ones.

After you wrap the yarn around the cardboard, cut it along the bottom of the board. Hold the cut strands together and fold them over. Slide the

Making fringe

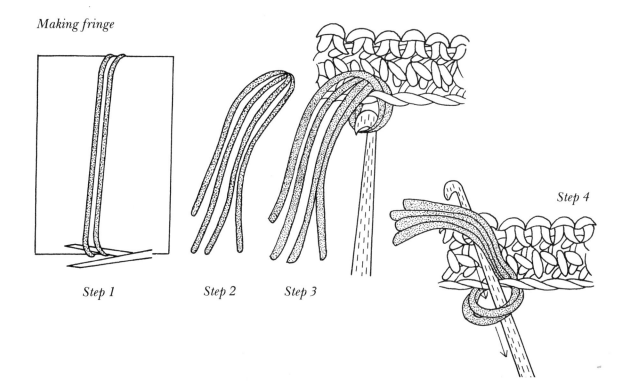

Step 1   *Step 2*   *Step 3*   *Step 4*

crochet hook into the material where you plan to attach a fringe. Catch all the yarn strands, and pull them through part way. Take the hook out of the loop, grab the cut ends with the hook and pull them through the big loop. Fasten any other fringes the same way, and give them a tug to tighten them.

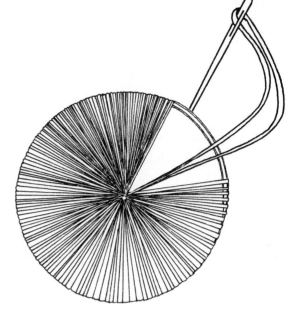

Making a pompon   *Step 1*

Pompons

Making pompons is just as easy and fun as making tassels. This time you'll need two little cardboard circles. The size of the pompons depends on the size of the cardboard circles. A four-inch circle will make a big pompon; a two-inch circle a smaller one. Plan how you want to use your pompon then make it to fit your design.

For this experiment we'll do a big pompon first. Cut two circles from soft cardboard that measure about four inches across. Hold the two circles together and punch a hole in the middle of both of them at the same time. Use a fat pencil to do this. Measure off a piece of yarn about 3 times the length of your arm and thread your yarn needle. Fold the yarn in half. Hold the 2 circles of cardboard together firmly so that one hole is directly over the other. Put the threaded needle through the holes and around the circles. Keep wrapping the yarn around the circles, through the holes, until the circles are completely covered and the holes are full.

Slip the scissors in between the 2 circles and snip the yarn all around

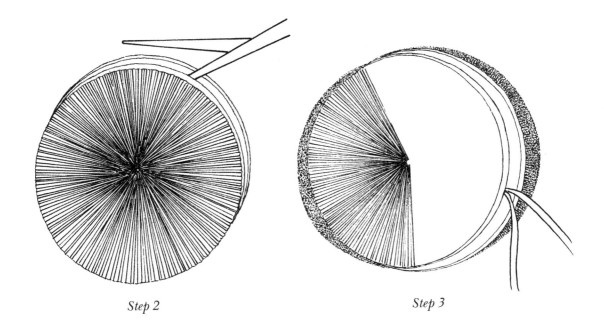

Step 2

Step 3

between the two circle edges. Slip another piece of yarn about half as long as your arm, between the 2 circles and wrap it around the center yarn about 6 times. Tie a firm knot. Remove the yarn from the cardboard. Shake the pompon then carefully trim any uneven ends. Leave one long yarn end so you can fasten the pompon to your design.

Make some pretend pompon flowers, and put them in a vase. These flowers will stay fresh forever. Every once in a while you should take them out of the vase and shake the dust off.

Crocheted Edge Decorations

A row or two of single or double crochet all around the outside edge of your work is an attractive way to decorate, and gives it a nicely finished look. Add some beads or buttons along the way.

Make a ruffled or wavy border by increasing *every other* stitch. If you have to turn a corner, make three stitches in one stitch. (Ovals, page 48.) For a deeper ruffle, increase in *every*

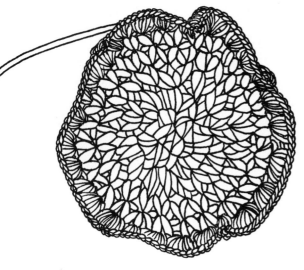

Single crocheted edge

stitch. The more border rows the bigger the ruffle. The object below started out to be a hat and ended up a bowl to display on a shelf. It's made from knitting worsted worked in single crochet. First a big circle was crocheted, then, working even (no increasing or decreasing), the crocheting was continued, round and round for about six inches. The ruffles were added later.

Page 77 shows Kaylynn wearing a big ruffled collar. Put it on your head, and presto! it's a big, floppy hat. When you're not wearing it use it for a centerpiece on the dining room table, or hang it on a wall. Ruffle your head with your own ideas.

Crocheted bowl with double ruffled edge

Kaylynn wearing a crocheted collar

Kaylynn turns her collar into a sun hat

Decorating With Chains

Gather up some practice yarn in as many colors as you can find. Make a big, long chain of one color—maybe about twice as long as your arm. Fasten off the last stitch. Make a second chain in another color, only this time a longer one. Make a bunch of chains —each a different color and length, and from different yarns.

Lay all the chains out side by side on a table. Arrange the colors to please you. Find a wire coat hanger, and tie each chain to the coat hanger, all along the bottom and up each side. (Page 61.) Hang it on your wall. Instant decoration!

Tie the ends of three of four chains together. Tie each bunch of chains to the coat hanger. Now you have another design.

Make a whole ceiling of chains like the kids at one school did. First, crochet a whole bunch of chains in lots of colors, or even all the same color. Then have someone help you tack them to the ceiling of your room. Be sure to get permission to put the tacks in the ceiling.

Find an embroidery hoop that no one's using—any size will do—then wrap the chains over and around the hoop. Tie each chain to the hoop as equally spaced as possible. Hang the hoop over your bed and you'll have a canopy.

Chains made from wool, cotton, linen and rope

Chains looped around embroidery hoops

19

Special Things to Make

Squares sewn together to make a box

Your crochet box must be overflowing with all the experiments you've been working on. Perhaps you've even displayed some of your handiwork. Now it's time to design and make something special and see if you can follow directions. So far you've learned how to begin and end, how to do a couple of crochet stitches, how to go around corners and make a lot of different shapes. You've learned something about colors and textures, too. Let's put all these bits and pieces together and try out the following projects.

Box It In

People like to keep their treasures in interesting boxes. They can be made of wood, cardboard, straw. But did you know you can crochet a box? Well, you can. The box can be a square, a rectangle, or even diamond-shaped. Your box can be any color or size you want. Each side a different color, or even another kind of yarn.

Let's try the square box first. You'll need to make six squares all the same size. Start with a chain about 6 inches long and single crochet back and forth until your work measures the same across and up and down. Fasten off the last stitch. Make 5 more squares the same size.

To assemble the box either crochet the parts or sew them together (Chap. 17). Let's sew this one. Pin 1 square to another, then overcast them with your big-eyed yarn needle. That takes care of 2 squares. Sew 3 more squares to the connected ones. One square will be the bottom of the box, the other 4 are the sides. Now you need a lid. Sew one edge of the last square to any side of a top edge. Now you have a square box with a lid. Make a fastener for the lid. Make a 6- or 7-stitch

chain and fasten off. Sew the chain to the center of one edge of the lid. Just below that, sew a button on and there's your treasure box!

Turn the box into a stuffed cube. After all the parts are sewn together except the 3 sides of the lid, stuff it with scraps of material or chopped up foam rubber. If you decide to use foam rubber, better spread some newspapers around because the foam rubber flies all over the place.

Stuff the box, so its good firm and sew the 3 remaining edges of the lid to the remaining edges of the box.

Do you think your box needs some decorations? How about gluing some interesting shells right onto the surface? Use instant glue to do this, but

Square box with lid—
overcast seams. Lid pinned,
ready to sew

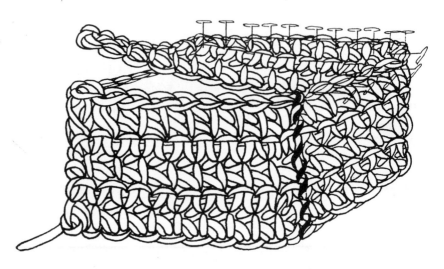

because it's a bit tricky to use, you'd better have an adult help you, or you could get your fingers stuck.

There are lots of other ways to decorate your box. Sew old buttons on, or add some fringe along the seams. You'll dream up other decorations as you work along.

Rectangle Box

The rectangle box is made just like the square box, except that the four sides are about twice as long as the top and bottom. Stuff it and stand it up on one end and it can be a pedestal or a building.

Make a whole bunch of boxes from other kinds of yarns or strings, in lots of colors. Stuff them and arrange them any way you like. You can even glue the boxes together.

Babies love to play with soft toys, so if you have a baby sister or brother, make a stuffed cube from washable knitting worsted. Babies like to put things in their mouths, so don't glue anything onto the outside for decoration. A baby could swallow a little shell or a bead. You can decorate it by weaving another color through the stitches. Here's how: Thread your

big-eyed yarn needle and weave the new yarn through every *other* stitch, along one row. Make some more rows the same way. Turn the cube around and weave some rows in the opposite direction. Weave in the ends of the yarn. You've made a pattern of plaid. Use other colors for a plaid pattern on the other sides of the cube.

These colorful boxes and cubes make great presents. If you don't have much money, crochet some boxes then fill the boxes with perfumed soap or wrapped candies, or cookies. I'll bet you know someone who would appreciate such a nice hand-made present.

Meet The Finger Folks

Do you and your friends like to put on puppet shows? Make a whole bunch of finger folks with silly hats and funny faces. Wag your fingers and make up some foolish words for each puppet. You and your friends can take turns. You'll need:

Kaylynn playing peek-a-boo with finger folks   *Back view of finger folks*

Leftover bright colored yarns
Crochet hook
Big-eyed yarn needle
Embroidery scissors
A little time
Some imagination

The bodies of the finger folks are little rectangles slip-stitched together. Make a 28-stitch chain. Crochet back and forth in single crochet until the rectangle fits around your finger. Slip stitch the 2 long edges together. Fasten off. Crochet 3 more rectangles, each another color, one for each finger. Crochet a shorter rectangle for your thumb.

Crochet a little circle for each rectangle. This will be the hat.

Girl puppets need hair, so cut 10 or

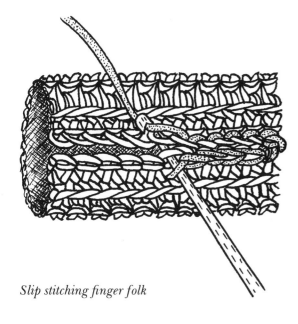

Slip stitching finger folk

shows are pretty popular with the kids.

When you are not playing with finger folks, leave them in a mug on your shelf so you'll always be able to find them.

Finger folks resting in a mug

12 pieces of yarn (any color), about 3 inches long. Lay the cut pieces of yarn over one end of the rectangle. Thread your yarn needle with matching yarn and sew the pieces to that end. If the hair seems a bit too long, trim the ends with the scissors.

With other colors of yarn, stitch on eyes, nose and mouth for each puppet. How about purple eyes, a green nose and a black mouth?

Now you're ready to have a puppet show. This is fun on a rainy day when you are tired of everything else and your mother wishes the rain would stop so you could go outside and play. It rains a lot in Seattle so puppet

Milk and cookies on a saucer

Milk and Cookies

Would you ever think you could crochet a glass of milk and some cookies? Of course you can. The photo shows a little glass of milk sitting on a saucer with an Oreo cookie and a chocolate chip cookie. The glass of milk is a crocheted circle combined with a plain old tunnel. The Oreo cookie is made from 3 circles stitched together and the chocolate chip cookie is another circle turned back on itself.

Here's what you'll need:

Some white knitting worsted
Some camel-colored string or yarn
A little bit of dark brown yarn
Some bright yarn for the saucer
Big-eyed yarn needle
Embroidery scissors
Crochet hook

For the milk, use the white yarn. Start with a 6-stitch chain, and connect it. Place a marker there.

Round 1. In single crochet, increase 1 stitch in every chain until you come back to the beginning.

Round 2. Increase 1 stitch in every *other* stitch.

Round 3. Increase 1 stitch in every *other* stitch.

Round 4. Work 1 round *even,* in the *back* loop of each stitch. This is the turning row and you are ready to start the main part of the glass.

Round 5. Decrease 3 stitches evenly spaced on this round.

Continue to *work even* on every round until the glass is four or 5 inches high.

Fasten off and weave in the tail.

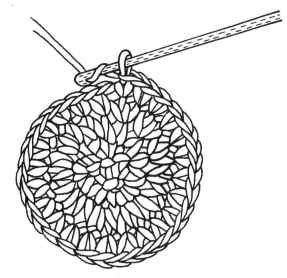

Single crocheting bottom of glass

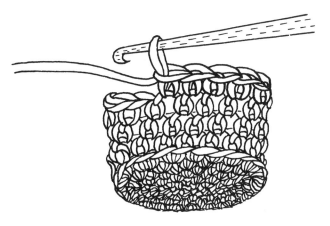

Crocheting the glass

CHOCOLATE CHIP COOKIE

With the camel colored string or yarn, make 6 chain stitches and connect them with a slip stitch.

Chocolate chip cookie

Round 1. Increase 1 stitch in *every* stitch.

Round 2. Increase 1 stitch in every *other* stitch.

Round 3. Increase 1 stitch in every *other* stitch.

Round 4. Increase 1 stitch in every *3rd* stitch.

Round 5. Work even.

Round 6. Increase 1 stitch in every *4th* stitch.

Round 7. Work even.

Round 8. Decrease 1 stitch in every *1th* stitch.

Round 9. Work even.

Continue to crochet around and around, decreasing stitches gradually until there are 2 stitches left. Fasten off and weave in the cut end.

To make the chocolate chips: Thread your big-eyed yarn needle with the dark brown yarn. On the top part of the cookie, catch a stitch with the tip of the needle and go in and out in the same stitch a couple of times. That's one chocolate chip.

Make some more chocolate chips in the same way. Do you like lots of chocolate chips? Make as many as you like.

OREO COOKIE

With the dark brown yarn make 2 circles the same size as the chocolate chip cookie, except this time fasten off after Round 7.

To make the vanilla filling, use the white yarn and make another circle, but fasten off after Round 6. Stack the three circles together like a sandwich, with the white circle between the two brown ones. Stitch them together in the middle, with the dark brown yarn. How's that for an Oreo?

Oreo cookie

SAUCER

Make a saucer for your milk and cookies by crocheting a great big circle. This time use two strands of the bright yarn together, and increase in every *other* stitch on every *other* round, until your saucer is large enough to hold the milk and cookies.

Fool everybody and put them on the table at dinner time!

Blow Your Horn

Start your own crocheted band. You can make a horn or a set of drums, or any other instruments you like. Use whatever yarns you have handy.

Here's how to make a horn: the horn is a long tube, with a big mouth. Start with a 12-stitch chain, and connect the 2 ends of the chain with a slip stitch. Work around even until you have a tube about 8 inches long. On the next round increase 1 stitch every fourth stitch. Work 1 round even. Continue to increase on 1 round, and *work even* 1 round, until your horn has a big wide mouth. Fasten off.

Make a handle for your trumpet. Chain 16 stitches, then crochet 1 single crochet stitch in each chain. Fasten

Blow your horn. Single crocheted from bright green knitting worsted, green tweed handle, old buttons for valves

off. Sew each end of the handle to the tube. Sew some buttons on the opposite side of the tube for the valves.

Now see if you can make some drums all by yourself.

Strawberry Ice Cream Cone

Everybody likes ice cream cones, and I bet you do, too. Here's one to crochet. Page 88 shows a strawberry ice cream cone, made from knitting worsted, and here's how to do it:

Strawberry ice cream cone—Cone single crocheted from camel color knitting worsted, with single crochet ridges; strawberry ice cream single crocheted from pink knitting worsted. Stuffed with old nylon pantyhose

CONE: Start with some camel-colored knitting worsted, or any other color. Beginning at the widest part, chain 20. Connect the 2 ends of the chain with a slip stitch in the usual way. On the next row, single crochet in the back of the stitch, and decrease 1 stitch every *fourth* stitch. Work 1 round even. Work this way, decreasing on one round and working even on the next, until you have 3 or 4

stitches left. Fasten off and weave the tail back into the cone.

STRAWBERRY ICE CREAM: With pink knitting worsted, make a circle that measures maybe 4 inches across. Leave about a 10-inch tail and cut all the yarn. Then gather the circle around the outside edge (as described for the Rectangle Hat on page 92). Before fastening off, stuff the circle with scraps of material or foam rubber bits, then tighten up the gathers and fasten off.

Stuff the cone with more scraps of material or foam rubber. Insert the ice cream into the wide part of the cone, and stitch it to the inside edge.

Crochet any other flavors you like, and serve them to company. Won't that be a surprise?

Instead of filling the cone with crocheted ice cream, turn it upside down and it's Mount St. Helens before the eruption. Stop crocheting before the tip of the cone and it's Mount St. Helens after the eruption!

20

Wear It

Have you had enough craziness for a while? How about making a fun sweater all by yourself? When you're not wearing it hang it on a hanger or display it on a wall in your room. This sweater is an easy one to make because there's no special shaping—just four rectangles either sewn together with your big-eyed needle and yarn, or crocheted together.

You'll need:

4—2 oz. balls of knitting worsted—each a different color, or all the same color
1 size K crochet hook
1 big-eyed yarn needle
T-pins
Tape measure

You can make all the rectangles in single crochet, or double crochet, or two in single crochet and two in double crochet, and alternate them. Just be sure all the pieces measure the same width and length. And you can arrange the colors however you want to. Page 90 shows Kaylynn wearing a

Rectangle sweater, single crocheted, decorated with pompons. (front)

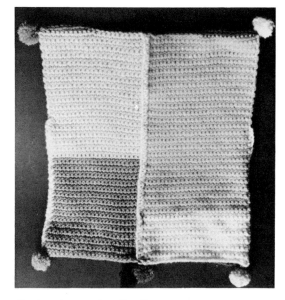

Rectangle sweater. (back)

and decide how long you want the sweater. Measure across your chest—from underarm to underarm. Ask an adult to help you. You're still growing, so add 2 inches to the chest measurement. Divide that measurement in half. For example, if your real measurement is 16 inches, add two more inches, then divide that number in half. Each rectangle should measure 9 inches across.

Start by crocheting a chain that measures 9 inches long. Work back

Kaylynn wearing her rectangle sweater (front view).

Kaylynn, back view

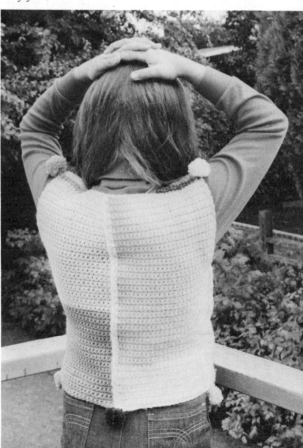

version of the rectangle sweater. The colors are white, yellow, pink, green, turquoise, and hot pink. The shoulders are crocheted together in hot pink and green, and the other seams in white. The tassels are made from all the colors. Notice that the colors of the rectangles don't all start and stop at the same place. Perhaps you'd like yours to look exactly like the picture.

First, take your measurements—width and length. Then hold the tape measure at the top of your shoulder and forth until your piece is as long as you want it to be. Fasten off. Make three more pieces the same way. Remember, your sweater can be all one color, or lots of colors, and you can start and stop the new color whenever you feel like doing so.

Here's how to connect the parts:

Step 1.   Pin the long edges of 2 rectangles together.

Step 2.   Single crochet the pinned edges, or overcast the pinned edges. (pages 68–70)

Fronts: Starting about 4 inches down (this is the neck opening), pin the other two rectangles together, then either crochet or sew them.

Shoulders: Measure about halfway across each shoulder starting from the armhole edge, and pin, then crochet or sew the back to the front.

Sides: Leave about 6 inches for the armhole measuring down from the shoulder. Pin, then crochet or sew the side seams.

Step 3

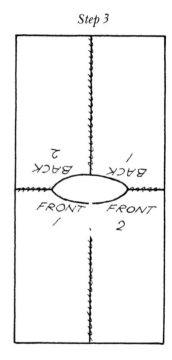

Connecting the rectangle sweater parts

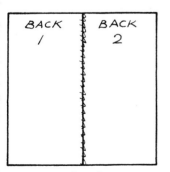

Step 1

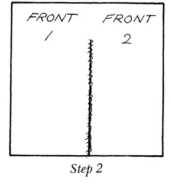

Step 2

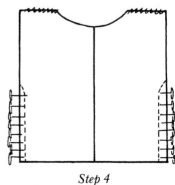

Step 4

Kaylynn wearing her rectangle hat

Weave in all the loose ends. Add some pompons or tassels for decoration. Or crochet a row of single crochet around the bottom, the armholes and around the neckline. Sew a button along one or both of the shoulder seams.

Check the drawings often to be sure that everything is OK.

When you get tired of this sweater, or grow out of it, unravel the yarn and make something else.

Rectangle Hat

Make a rectangle hat to wear on a cold winter's day. The hat on page 94 is a crocheted rectangle. The short ends of the rectangle were sewn together, then gathered at one end. A pompon decorates the top of the hat. This hat is made from three colors of leftover knitting worsted in yellow, green and white. You can make it all the same color or lots of colors.

You'll need:

2 oz. of knitting worsted
1 size H crochet hook
T-pins
Big-eyed yarn needle

Crochet a chain of 36 stitches. Work back and forth in single crochet until the rectangle fits around your head. Fasten off the last stitch, but this time leave about a 15-inch tail. Thread your yarn needle with the long tail. Starting one row down from one edge weave the needle in and out,

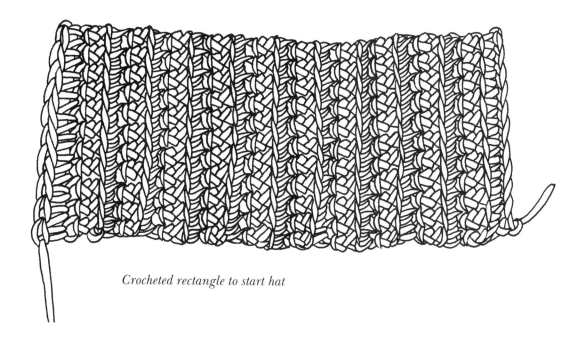

Crocheted rectangle to start hat

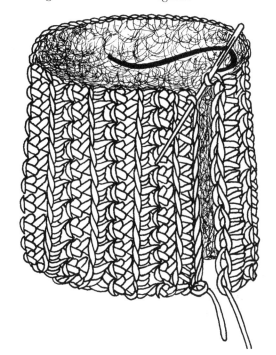

Sewing the two short ends together

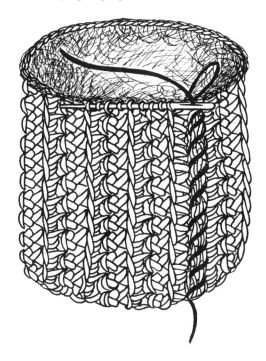

Gathering top edge of hat.

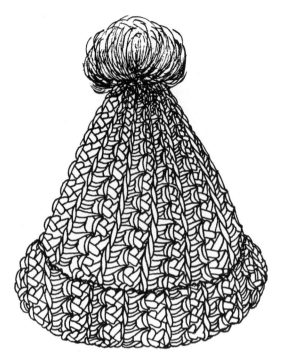

Finished hat with pompon decoration.

Braided Belt

Crochet a chain long enough to fit around your waist, plus 7 or 8 more inches. Work one row of single crochet. Fasten off. Make two more the same length.

Tie all three chains together in a knot at one end. Start braiding them at the knotted end. Tie them together at the other end. Wear your braided belt with your jeans. Make a bunch of belts to wear with other things.

Braided belt made with single crocheted chains (right.)

Chain stitch bracelet with inserted beads (left)

working from right to left, until you come back to the starting point. Pull the yarn up until the edge is tightly gathered. Go over the last stitch two or three times to anchor the stitch so it doesn't work loose. Cut the yarn and weave the end back into the material. Make a tassel or pompon to decorate your hat, and that's all there is to it.

Make some rectangle hats for presents for your family or for special friends. Won't you be proud?

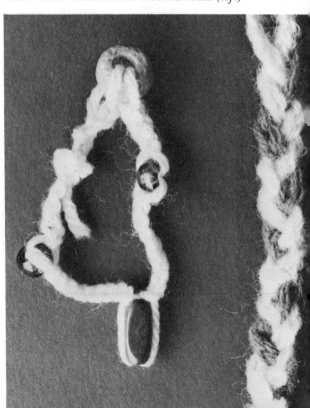

Braided belt

Beaded Bracelet

Here's another suggestion for using up leftovers and combining them with beads. Make a pretty bracelet.

Crochet a chain long enough to fit around your wrist. Add a bead every few stitches. (Page 64.) Fasten off the last stitch, and there's your instant bracelet.

Make a longer chain, and turn the bracelet into a necklace. Invent some other kinds of soft jewelry.

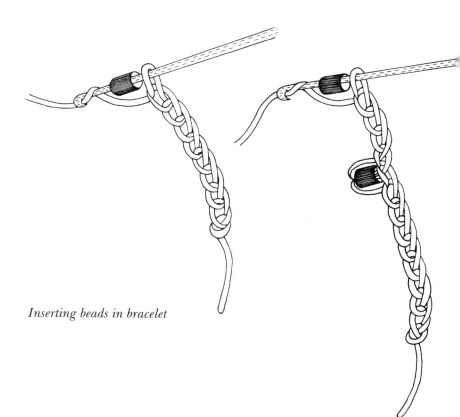

Inserting beads in bracelet

21

A Little Starch Helps

Last, but not least, here's one more idea that might be useful to try when your designs need a little firming up. Put some liquid starch in a spray bot-

Mr. Rat—Single crocheted of orange knitting worsted, with pink ears, black whiskers

Abstract shape using leftover yarns in single and double crochet. Made by University Heights Student

tle and lightly spray your design. Better do this in the garage or carport (if you have one), or outside in the backyard. Be sure the starch is completely dry before you handle your creation.

By now I hope you have enjoyed all the experiments in this book and can understand the whole idea of crazy crochet . . . that you can create anything you want to with a ball of yarn and a crochet hook, or just your fingers.

Let your imagination fly, and soon your fingers will, too!

Index

The chain gang—Eric, Mason and Chris

I

J

K

L

M

N

O

P

Tooth crocheted by May Chin. Made from knitting worsted. Single crochet. Filling in gold, tooth in off-white

T

W

Y